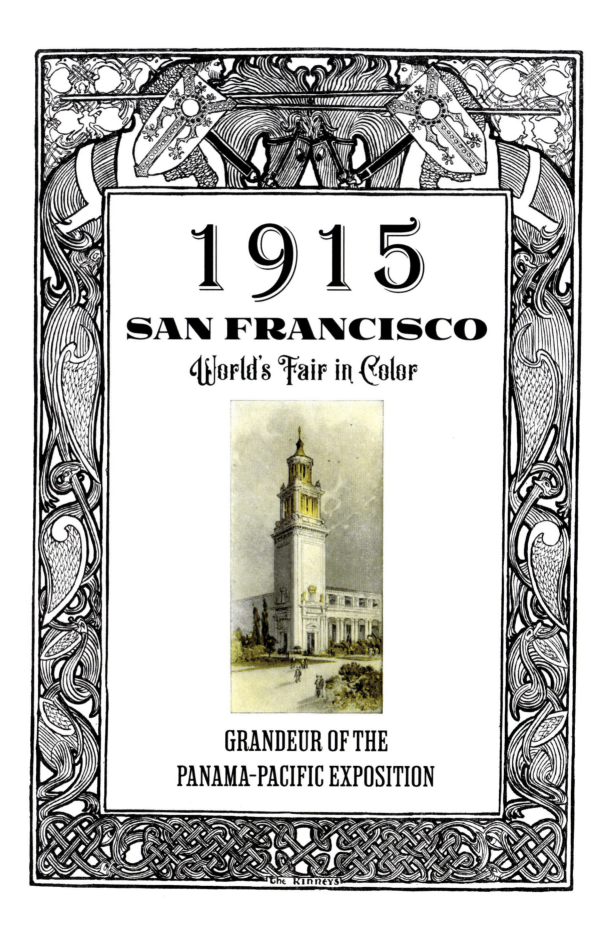

1915
SAN FRANCISCO
World's Fair in Color

**GRANDEUR OF THE
PANAMA-PACIFIC EXPOSITION**

1915 San Francisco World's Fair in Color:
Grandeur of the Panama-Pacific Exposition

Written by Mark Bussler

Copyright © 2021 Inecom, LLC.
All Rights Reserved

No parts of this book may be reproduced or broadcast in any
way without written permission from Inecom, LLC.

www.CGRpublishing.com

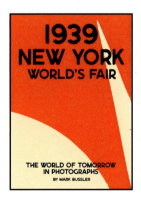
1939 New York World's Fair:
The World of Tomorrow in
Photographs

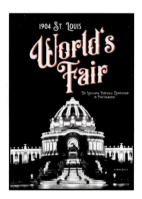
1904 St. Louis World's Fair: The
Louisiana Purchase Exposition in
Photographs

The World's Fair of 1893 Ultra
Massive Photographic Adventure
Series

The Tower of Jewels.

INTRODUCTION

California hosted the 1915 San Francisco World's Fair from February 20 to December 4, 1915, during a time of great change in the United States and the world.

The Panama-Pacific International Exposition took place 50 years after the American Civil War, roughly 20 years after the Columbian Exposition in Chicago, and about a decade after the 1904 World's Fair in St. Louis. San Francisco had only recently survived a devastating earthquake in 1906 that nearly destroyed the entire city.

In 1915, electricity was still in its infancy, as was the automobile industry. Air travel was a new and exciting marvel, and so were motion pictures. The Great War broke out a year earlier in Europe, though, at the time, nobody imagined how bad it would get.

Woodrow Wilson was the 28th President, and most of the 48 states in the United States participated in the Exposition, including the territories of Alaska and Hawaii. More than 18 million people visited the Exposition, and promenaded through the lush fairgrounds and reveled in The Zone.

Though largely taken for granted today, the Exposition celebrated the completion of the Panama Canal, one of the most significant engineering projects in history. The Panama Canal revolutionized global maritime travel and trade by practically connecting the Atlantic and the Pacific Oceans, saving ships the lengthy and hazardous trip around the tip of South America.

One of the guidebooks from the event says, "it is the most remarkable achievement of man, not only because of the great engineering ability and the vast financial outlay involved in its construction but because humanity, man's consideration for his fellow man, has so progressed that now the deadly miasmas of the tropics are nullified and the battle lost to climatic and physical conditions is turned to victory by the science of hygienic sanitation."

"The Panama Canal is a monument to the humanitarian forces of the world which combined with those of the United States to accomplish now what a few decades ago was a practical impossibility. Therefore, it is pre-eminently proper that the official festivities celebrating the completion and opening of the Canal be so planned that all nations and peoples may participate and display their choicest products to demonstrate by examples understandable regardless of the language, the mental, the moral, and material condition of the world in 1915, four hundred years after Balboa discovered the Pacific Ocean."

I sourced the imagery and writing in this book from contemporary guidebooks created during and before the Exposition, and based the writing style on their enthusiastic and often boastful pride in the event. Please enjoy a colorful trip to the 1915 World's Fair through the eyes of those who were there and in the words that they wrote about the Panama-Pacific International Exposition.

- Mark Bussler

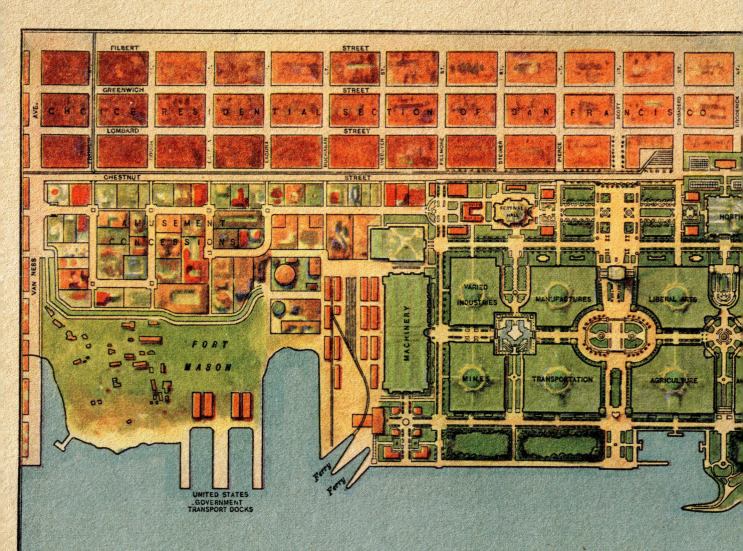

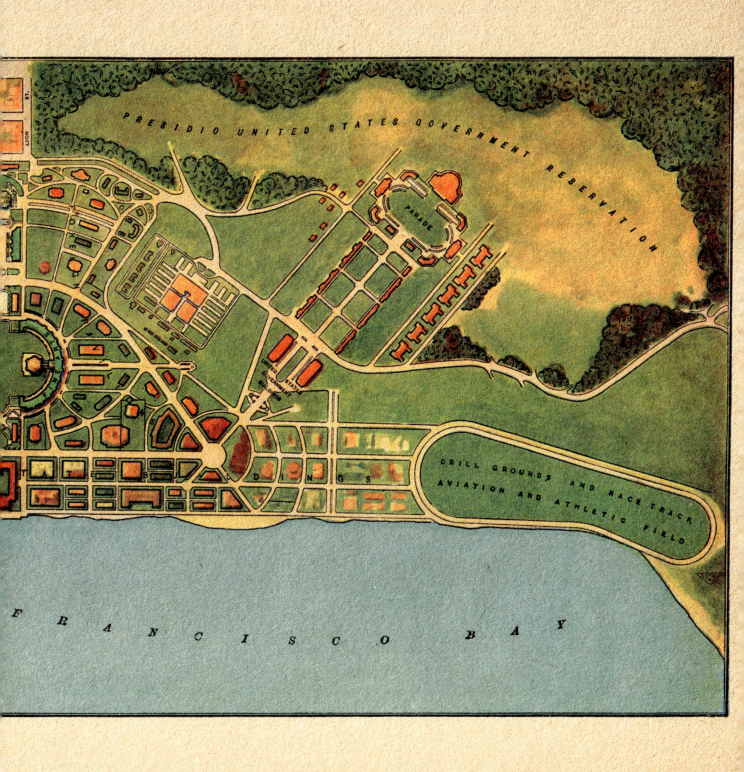

THE COLUMN OF PROGRESS

THE COLUMN OF PROGRESS

Dominating the picture in the center foreground is the colossal Column of Progress. It stands on the esplanade in front of the northern extension of the Court of the Universe. The beautiful bas-reliefs around the base of the column are the work of Isadore Konti of New York.

Around the column from the base to the crown is a spiral design of a ship on the ocean, representing man's voyages of discovery. Capping the column are H. A. McNeill's Burden Bearers, supporting the Adventurous Bowman, who has just shot the Arrow of Success towards the west.

Rising to a height of 260 feet, it is a very imposing and impressive sight. It is one of the four colossal pieces of sculpture on the grounds of the Exposition, the other three being, respectively, Nations of the East, Nations of the West, and the Fountain of Energy.

THE SOUTH GARDENS (EAST)

The spread on pages 12 and 13 features a beautiful picture of the great South Gardens looking east from the Palace of Horticulture. It is a characteristic image, as it shows the arrangement of the French and Italian formal gardens and the beds with their golden blaze of tulips surrounding one of the pools.

On the extreme right of the picture is the Press Building, home of the Press Club, and host building to the visiting newspaper and magazine men. Next to it is the beautiful Festival Hall, designed by Robt. Farquhar of Los Angeles.

Partially hiding the view of Festival Hall is Calder's famous Fountain of Energy. Towards the left of the picture are seen Kelham's two Italian towers marking the entrance to the Court of Flowers.

Continuing to the left of the picture, we pass the Palace of Manufactures and come to the base of the Tower of Jewels. This picture was taken in April and, as the shadows denote, on one of California's many sunny days well towards evening.

FOUNTAIN OF ENERGY IN SOUTH GARDENS AT NIGHT
PAN. PAC. INT. EXPOSITION
SAN FRANCISCO, 1915

THE PANAMA-PACIFIC EXPOSITION

(Based on text from the Official Panama-Pacific International Exposition Illustrated)

The Panama-Pacific International Exposition celebrates the completion of that epochal achievement, the Panama Canal. It also celebrates the achievements of mankind during the decade preceding the year 1915 and shows the great progress that has been made in every branch of human endeavor.

The Exposition grounds, containing 635 acres, are in a natural amphitheater overlooking San Francisco Bay and extend something over two miles along the waterfront, affording unobstructed views of naval pageants and other aquatic features. The magnificent structures which house the evidences of the world's progress rise majestic in their grandeur; their capacity is enormous, and their sculptural decorations are symbolic of the exhibits they contain.

These exhibits are divided into eleven groups: Fine Arts; Education and Social Economy; Liberal Arts; Manufactures, Varied Industries; Machinery; Transportation; Agriculture; Live Stock; Horticulture, and Mines and Metallurgy. The exhibit of the Government is divided into sections representing all of the executive departments, State, Treasury, War, Post Office, Navy, Interior, Agriculture and Commerce and Labor.

The method of lighting employed on the exposition grounds is known as the "indirect method"; the walls of the exhibit palaces being bathed by the light from great arcs. The domes of the buildings are flooded with light from powerful searchlights, and their rays fall upon the "jewels" of hand-cut crystal.

At no exposition has there been so elaborate and extensive a floral display as shown at this exposition. The main avenues are featured with large specimen trees and palms. Against the great Exhibit Palaces have been planted cypress, spruce, eucalyptus, fir, and other species, from twenty to thirty feet high. Next, there are trees and shrubbery of lesser height, and these are banked with flowers of brilliant hue. For nearly a mile along the bay frontage stretches the North Gardens.

The South Gardens embrace the entire territory between the Horticultural Building and Festival Hall. The main central court of the Exposition, or Court of the Universe, is distinguished by a formal setting of shrubbery in the center of which is a large sunken garden. Myrtle hedges, pillar roses, and climbing plants are freely used in the adornment of this court. In the Court of Abundance may be seen among other things one hundred orange trees in bearing.

In the Court of Palms are different varieties of palms and a collection of sweet-smelling shrubs. The Court of Flowers, as the name denotes, will be a showing of brilliantly hued flowers in great variety. The Court of the Four Seasons is laid out to illustrate the various phases of the four seasons and is graced with groups of statuary representing Spring, Summer, Autumn, and Winter. The exhibit palaces are shaded in neutral tint-smoked ivory. The portals, colonnades, and groupings of architectural features are massed in reds, blues, greens, and gold.

The following foreign countries have officially accepted the invitation of the United States Government to participate in the Exposition: Guatemala, Haiti, Salvador, Dominican Republic, Honduras, Panama, Mexico, Peru, Costa Rica, Bolivia, Japan, Ecuador, Uruguay, Canada, Liberia, France, Nicaragua, Cuba, China, Portugal, Sweden, Netherlands, Argentine, Denmark, Chile, Brazil, Venezuela, Persia, Paraguay, New Zealand, Turkey, Australia, Italy, Siam, Greece, Austria, Switzerland, Norway, Monaco, Bulgaria, Serbia. Forty-three of the States of the Union are participating

All of the State buildings are handsome structures, large and commodious, exceedingly creditable to the States. Alaska, Hawaii, and the Philippines each give the visitor an opportunity to become familiar with the character of these countries, their people, and manner of life.

The amusement section of the Exposition has been named "The Zone"! From the Avenue of Progress, near the Fillmore Street entrance, The Zone extends east for a distance of three thousand feet, equal to seven city blocks. Upon both sides of the thoroughfare, the amusement palaces and show houses line the way. Some of the attractions are the Panama Canal, Creation, the Grand Canyon of Arizona, the Yellowstone Park, the Chinese Village, Toyland Grown Up, the '49 Camp, the Dayton Flood, the Irish Village, the L. A. Thompson's Scenic Railway,

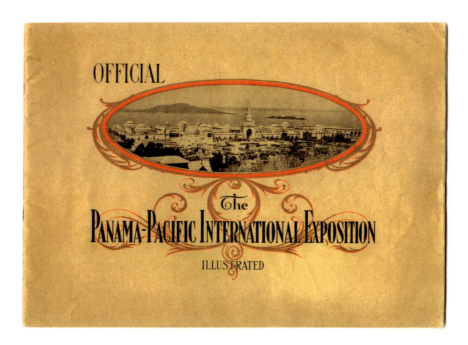

the Baby Incubator, the Evolution of the Dreadnaught, the Submarines, Japan Beautiful, the Battle of Gettysburg, the Diving Girls and Neptune's Daughters, Alligator Joe's Farm, the Old Mill, Mahomet's Mountain, Narren Pallast or Foolish House, and a great number of other attractions.

Aviation has been given much attention, and the aviation field will be found filled with hangars, slides, runways, sheds, and other necessary buildings for the accommodation of the "sky fleet." The Exposition Stadium, a specially prepared track, with all the improvements known in the athletic arena, attracts the world's greatest athletes, and competitions are held daily.

The University Greek Theatre at Berkeley, Stanford University's spacious buildings, and the new Auditorium in the Civic Center, seating 10,000, and erected at the cost of over one million dollars, are at the disposal of many congresses and conventions to be held during the Exposition.

San Francisco has over two thousand hotels, apartments, and rooming houses, with eight hundred restaurants and cafes. Over ninety percent are new and possess all modern conveniences. Oakland, Alameda, and Berkeley can care for about seventy-five thousand visitors.

FACTS ABOUT CALIFORNIA AND SAN FRANCISCO IN 1915

(Based on text from the Official Panama-Pacific International Exposition Illustrated)

Today it is difficult to believe that in 1906 San Francisco was in ruins. Its principal business, theater, hotel, and residential sections were destroyed by fire. The present city built on the ruins, evidences courage, energy, and resourcefulness which demand admiration and inspire confidence.

Those who faced calamity saw their homes and properties to the value of $700,000,000 disappear in flames, but who, never faltering, brought order out of chaos and then built a city better, safer, and more commodious than its predecessor, may safely be counted upon to construct and operate an exposition which will worthily celebrate the completion of the Panama Canal, and in which all peoples may participate with full confidence that the management is honest, able and efficient.

California is about 780 miles in length, and in width varies from 150 to 300 miles. Its area is 158,097 square miles, or approximately the total area of Maine, New Hampshire, Vermont, Massachusetts, Rhode Island, Connecticut, New York, and Pennsylvania. It is nearly 50 percent larger than Austria, Hungary, or Italy and barely 20 percent smaller than France or Germany. Its physical geography is boldly simple. The Sierras on the east and the Coast Ranges on the west enclose the Sacramento and San Joaquin Valleys, which form the Great Valley, 450 miles long and averaging 40 miles broad, with a single drainage gap to the Pacific Ocean through San Pablo and San Francisco Bays.

California climate is mild and uniform, but local conditions and elevations furnish almost any desired temperature from that on the peak of Mount Whitney, 14,502 feet above sea level, to that in the Colorado Desert, depressed 276 feet below sea level.

Alcatraz Island and San Francisco Bay from the Exposition.

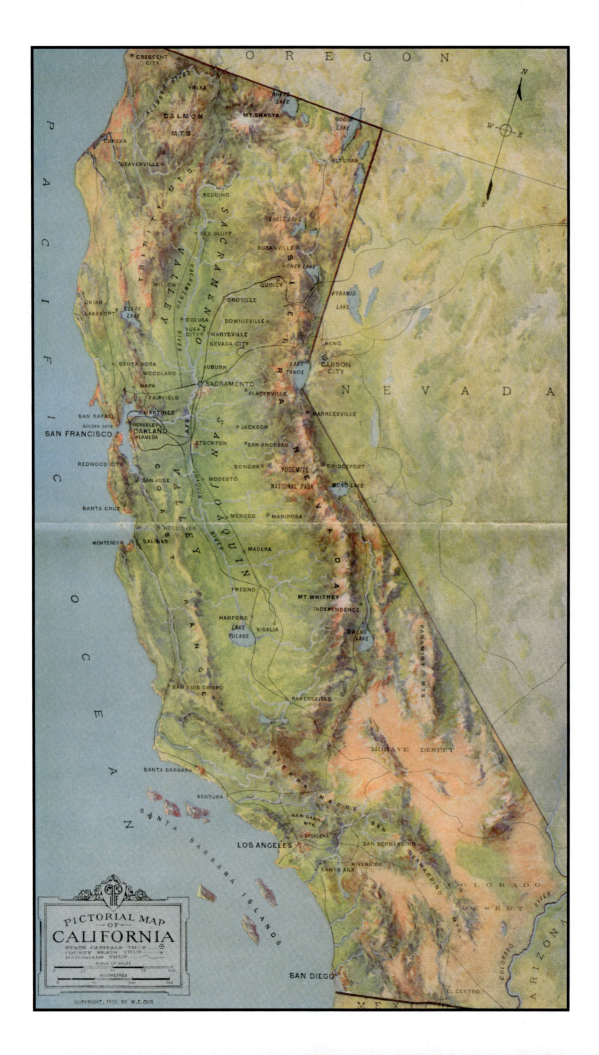

Fertile valleys of extreme beauty and productivity are frequent in the slopes of the Coast Ranges, and the deserts in the South are being reclaimed by scientific irrigation.

Can San Francisco take care of the crowds at the Exposition? Yes, with ease, in a manner, and at prices to suit the tastes and pocketbooks of all. Its population, location, surroundings, and climate combine to make San Francisco one of the most cosmopolitan, hospitable, and elastic of cities. There a dinner may be ordered in any language, found true to the characteristics desired in substance and service, but reasonable in cost since California produces the counterparts for the meats, fish, vegetables, and fruits of every clime.

San Franciscans are pleasure-loving, and when their city is *en fete* they evidence and diffuse the infectious carnival spirit of southern Europe. Their attitude toward strangers is habitually kindly and hospitable. Topographic and climatic conditions provide an almost unlimited range from which to select living quarters in and near San Francisco: city, village, rural, seashore, or mountain-camp life is available, and all are made comfortably accessible from the Exposition by excellent transportation facilities on land or water.

Clockwise from top: Mirror Lake in the Yosemite - The Beach, Seal Rocks, and Cliff House in San Francisco - "Stopped by the California Coast 7,000 Miles from Asia"

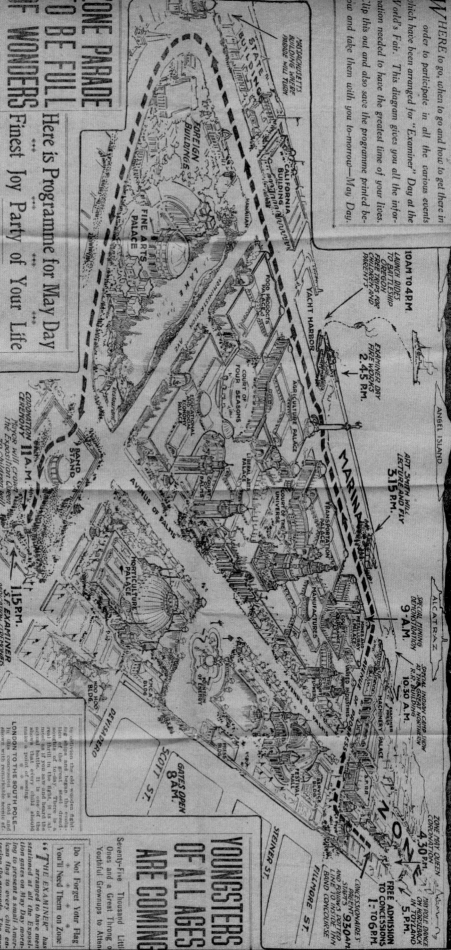

Contemporary Newspaper Clipping and Rare Map of the Exposition.

THE SOUTH GARDENS (WEST)

THE SOUTH GARDENS (WEST)

A gorgeous picture of the great South Gardens, looking west from Festival Hall. To the extreme right of the picture rises the Tower of Jewels, the dominant architectural feature of the main group of exhibit palaces and the center of its brilliant night illumination.

There are 125,000 "Novagems," or hand-cut jewels hung tremulously upon the Tower, so that the slightest breeze makes them flash and sparkle and scintillate like myriads of diamonds, emeralds, and rubies. The Tower, which favors the Aztec school of architecture, is 433 feet high and is the design of Messrs. Carrere & Hastings of New York.

Following the facade of the Palace of Liberal Arts to the center of the picture, we come to Geo. C. Kelham's two Italian towers, each 200 feet in height, marking the entrance to the Court of Flowers.

On the left is shown the great glass dome of the Palace of Horticulture, designed by Messrs. Bakewell & Brown of San Francisco. This palace covers over five acres of ground, and the great dome is 160 feet in height. John McLaren directed the landscaping.

The most imposing single architectural feature of the Exposition is the Tower of Jewels. The Tower has a mighty steel frame within, and its pillared and sculptured exterior is wonderfully impressive in the light of day.

At night the Tower sparkles with a hundred thousand jewels in the light of powerful electric rays. It rises to 433 feet and serves as the main entrance to the Court of the Universe. The Tower was erected by Commary-Peterson Company, after designs by Carrere & Hastings of New York.

The Tower of Jewels
and the Great South Gardens

COURT OF THE UNIVERSE

COURT OF THE UNIVERSE

This is the Grand Central Court or Court of Honor of the Exposition. It was designed by Messrs. McKim, Meade & White of New York, and the architecture is all of the Italian Renaissance period. Its symbolism represents the center of the Universe, the meeting place of the Eastern and Western Hemispheres.

From north to south, this court is 700 feet, and from east to west it is 900 feet. The Court of Honor has a sunken garden in the center and four enormous crescent-shaped rhododendron beds, which from May to September are a glorious blaze of color.

To the right of the picture is shown the Triumphal Arch of the Rising Sun, surmounted by the statuary group, Nations of the East. This is balanced on the west by the Arch of the Setting Sun, surmounted by the statuary group called Nations of the West. There are also two beautiful fountains in this court, the one to the left of the picture is the Fountain of the Setting Sun, and the one to the right the Fountain of the Rising Sun.

AVENUE OF PALMS

Next to The Zone, the Avenue of Palms is the most popular thoroughfare of the Exposition. It has been said that this is the most beautiful mile walk in the world today. Starting from the Avenue of Progress, a point just out of the right-hand corner of the picture, The Avenue of Palms passes on the right successively the Palace of Varied Industries with its wonderful doorway, the Court of Flowers, the Palace of Manufactures, the Tower of Jewels, the Palace of Liberal Arts, the Court of Palms, and the Palace of Education, terminating at the band concourse into the Avenue of the Nations.

On the left is passed the ornate Festival Hall, the great South Gardens, and the glass-domed Palace of Horticulture. It is truly a royal roadway filled with entrancing beauties and worldwide wonders. The entire facade along the right, including the ornamental doorways and the various vending kiosks (excepting the Tower of Jewels,) is the design of Messrs. Bliss & Faville, architects of San Francisco.

AVENUE OF PALMS

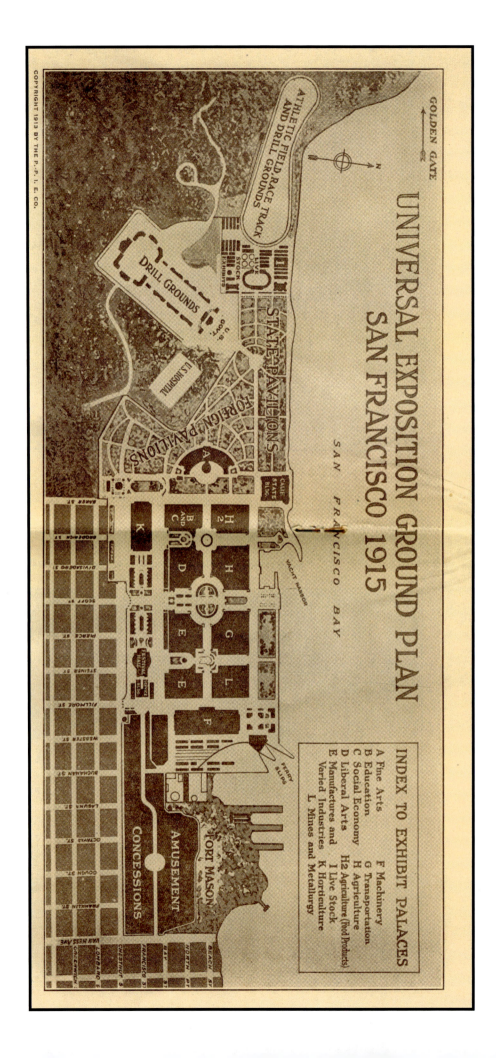

Great South Gardens.

FESTIVAL HALL

FESTIVAL HALL

The view shown here is the western entrance to Festival Hall. This palace is the host of the great symphony concerts, organ and harp recitals, and vocal renditions during the Exposition period. The great organ built inside is the seventh-largest in the world. Recitals are given almost daily by the leading organists of the time.

Festival Hall is a good example of the French theater style of architecture, having one large central dome and four smaller domes or minarets, the peaks of which are decorated with statuary.

Festival Hall sits at the eastern end of the South Garden, opposite the Court of Flowers (one of the towers at the entrance can be seen at the left of the picture) in juxtaposition to the Palace of Horticulture, which is opposite the Court of Palms. The main hall has a seating capacity of 3,000 persons. Robert Farquhar of Los Angeles is the designer.

Festival Hall fronts upon the South Gardens, at the right of the Main Entrance, and faces the Palace of Horticulture which it somewhat resembles in its circular form of architecture. Its daily occupation for congresses, conventions, concerts, and other musical features, causes it to be one of the most important and popular buildings upon the exposition grounds. Mr. R. D. Farquhar, was its architect, and it was built by McLaren & Peterson.

Night Illumination of the South Gardens: The illuminating system adopted at the Exposition is the culminating example of recent attainment in lighting great areas,

Bird's Eye View of the Exposition: Near the center may be seen the Tower of Jewels and the Court of the Universe. Around them are grouped the various exhibit palaces, Machinery Palace being farthest to the right, with "The Zone," or amusement street just beyond. The Palace of Fine Arts, at the left, forms a division between the group of exhibit palaces and the sections devoted to Foreign Pavilions and State Buildings.

PALACE OF FINE ARTS

PALACE OF FINE ARTS

Probably if man had striven for a century, he could not have designed a more beautiful or fitting storehouse for the art gems of the world than the Palace of Fine Arts. Beautiful in design, color, situation, and surroundings, it invariably elicits an exclamation of surprised delight from even the most callous and blasé traveler.

The palace proper is in the form of an arc 1100 feet long, placed in the center of which is a domed temple. The palace was designed by R. B. Maybeck of Berkeley, Cal., and is an example of Greek and Roman architecture. The classic domed temple in the center of the picture reminds one of a mausoleum or tomb of a Grecian Emperor.

The placid lagoon provides a perfect setting.

COLONNADES OF THE PALACE

The walk herewith shown is part of the 1100-foot avenue between the colonnades of the Palace of Fine Arts that surround the Temple of Art.

No true lover of art or student of the sublime works of man or Nature can walk here without being deeply impressed or without gaining great inspiration. The massive, fluted jade and sienna columns with their ornate capitals, the dark rose tint of the interior walls, the shrubbery, the bronze and marble statuary, and the blue sky all blend here to make a picture that is at once entrancing, soulful, and awe-inspiring. The beauty of the Palace of Fine Arts has never before been equaled.

Inside the Palace has been gathered one of the greatest collections of art subjects ever assembled in one place. It represents varied artwork from around the globe.

COLONNADES OF THE PALACE

THE GOLDEN GATE FROM THE TOWER OF JEWELS

The view on the previous page is from the beautiful Tower looking towards the Golden Gate. From the days of the gold discovery, this great waterway has been famed in song and story as the pathway to a haven of plenty, and every ray of the sunset scene has been interwoven with golden threads of hope and promise.

In the distance on the left is seen Fort Winfield Scott, with Fort Point on the right, government fortifications guarding the Golden Gate. In the foreground are the great exhibit palaces of the Exposition. More distant from left to right are the Fine Arts Palace, Argentina's beautiful pavilion, Oregon's unique state building, and many other State and foreign buildings beyond.

The Palace of Liberal Arts and Calder's Fountain of Energy.

THE FOUNTAIN OF ENERGY

The view on the previous page is a scene looking from the base of the Tower of Jewels towards the residence section of San Francisco.

In the center of the South Gardens, just inside the main Exposition entrance from the city side and directly opposite the Tower of Jewels stands Calder's impressive creation, the Fountain of Energy.

Its symbolism, freely translated, is as follows: The heroic figure on horseback typifies Man's Energy triumphant over all difficulties in his endeavor to divide the continents and unite the oceans. The two figures on his broad shoulders symbolize Communication East and West.

In the pool beneath the globe are four aquatic figures representing the Atlantic, the Pacific, the North Sea, and the South Sea. There are twelve smaller figures, three at each of the four corners, and they are conventional dolphins with Neptune's sons and daughters riding them with graceful pose.

Fountain of the Setting Sun in the Court of the Universe.

PALACE OF HORTICULTURE

PALACE OF HORTICULTURE

The Palace of Horticulture is a rather faithful example of the Saracenic school of architecture. It stands proudly in its setting of evergreen shrubbery and gorgeous flower beds. With its duplicate image reflected in the clear waters of the pool, it presents one of the most perfect of a long list of beautiful Exposition pictures.

The six obelisks (or spires) give character to the edifice and fit in well with the great dome, which rises to a height of 160 feet. The general ornamentation, while seeming to be rather extravagant, consistently follows the theme of a bounteous harvest and forms a fitting exterior to a palace designed to house the horticultural exhibits of the earth.

This beautiful palace is also the largest of its kind in the world. Messrs. Bakewell & Brown of San Francisco are the architects.

An Exposition Audience in the Great South Gardens.

Palm Avenue

Aerial View of the Palace of Horticulture.

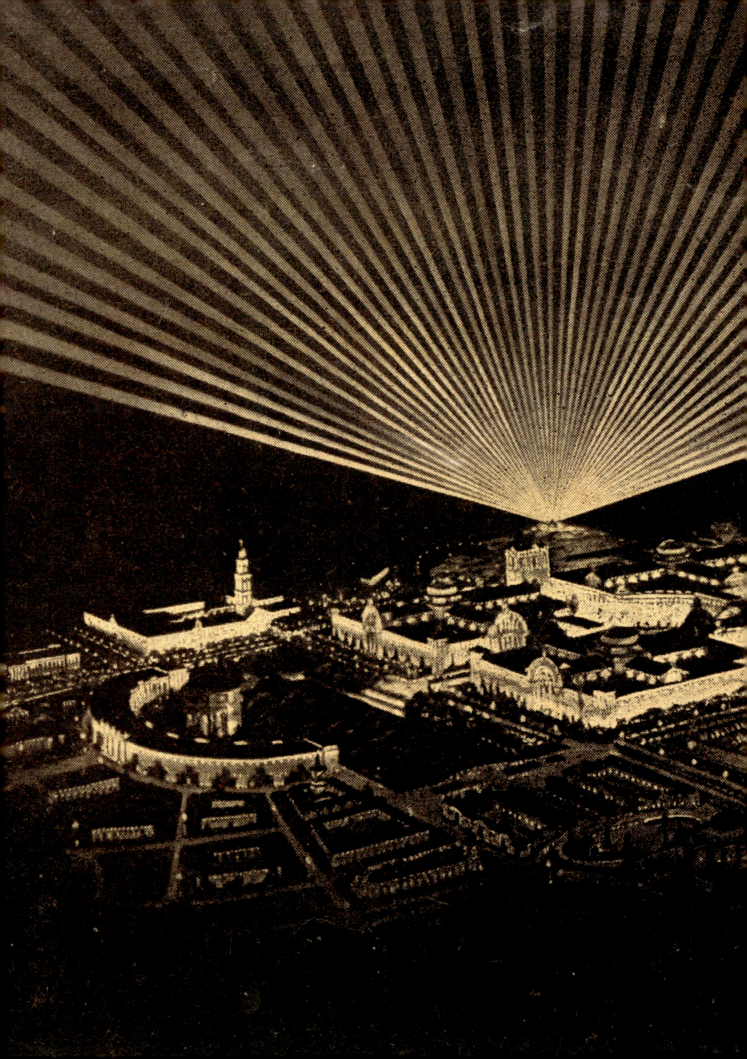

ARCH AND FOUNTAIN OF THE SETTING SUN

The Triumphal Arch of the Nations of the West stands at the western entrance of the Court of the Universe. The structure surmounted by the winged figure is one of the most beautiful pieces of statuary on the grounds. It is called the Fountain of the Setting Sun.

The group of statuary atop the arch is typical of the Nations of the West. The statuary depicts an old prairie schooner in the center, which balances the elephant on the top of the other arch standing across from it.

The soft, pastel color scheme of the Exposition is beautifully carried out in this court. One hundred and ten Corinthian columns surround the area, back of which is a broad vestibule, allowing plenty of room to promenade in the event of inclement weather.

Band concerts, exquisite flower beds, and playing fountains make this a favorite resting place for the visitor. Under this arch, two of DuMond's wonderful murals are hung. McKim, Meade & White of New York are the architects.

ARCH AND FOUNTAIN OF THE RISING SUN

The panoramic picture on the next page features the Triumphal Arch of the Nations of the East at the eastern entrance to the Court of the Universe. The structure to the left surmounted by the winged figure is that of the Fountain of the Rising Sun.

This picture was taken in early spring when the rhododendron beds were ablaze. Some idea of the magnificent plan on which this court was laid out can be had from an observance of the comparative size of the people on the steps.

The Court of the Universe is designed to be the meeting place of the Eastern and Western Hemispheres. The group of statuary on top of the arch is typical of the nations of the East, which man looks upon as the place where the sun rises. In this vast space, two hundred thousand people can congregate without undue crowding.

Two of Edward Simmons' murals adorn the walls under the mosaic dome of the arch. McKim, Meade & White of New York are the designers of this court.

SECTION OF COURT OF SUN AND STARS

In its center the court will contain a sunken garden, and in its northern axis, between the Agricultural and Transportation Buildings, will be a great pool of water embellished with statuary and fountains and bordered by tropical growth.

COURT OF THE FOUR SEASONS

The Court of the Four Seasons besides being the most delicately beautiful part of the Exposition's color scheme contains some very striking examples of modern statuary by Furio Piccirilli and Albert Jaegers. Harvest, Sunshine and Rain are by Jaegers and Spring, Summer, Autumn and Winter are by Piccirilli. Milton Bancroft's four great murals-Seed Time, Fruition, Harvest and Festivity-also adorn this court. Coming from the court through the aisle of Spring, which is the connecting avenue between the Palaces of Education and Food Products, a very beautiful vista of the Lagoon and Temple of Art is to be enjoyed. The inscriptions greeting the visitor in the court upon entrance and departure are most poetic, and suggestive of the surroundings. The beautiful Fountain of Ceres in the northern extension of this court is by Mrs. Evelyn Longman.

THE FOUNTAIN OF CERES AND COURT OF THE FOUR SEASONS

In the center foreground is the Fountain of Ceres, the work of Mrs. Evelyn Longman. In the center background is the mosaic-vaulted half dome surmounted by Albert Jaeger's Harvest and, topping the sienna columns on either side, are Sunshine and Rain by the same sculptor.

Stretching diagonally across the four corners are colonnaded niches containing statuary figures typical of the seasons. Beautifully appropriate inscriptions are placed over the eastern and western entrance ways.

This court was designed by Henry Bacon of New York, who received his inspiration from Hadrian's Villa, a noble Roman palace. Tinted by the master hand of Jules Guerin and planted by the wizard, John McLaren, as one enters the quiet precincts of this court, bathed in California sunshine, there comes a feeling of peace, contentment, and eternal spring.

Fountain of Ceres, Court of Four Seasons. Pan. Pac. Int. Expo.

ILLUMINATION, COURT OF THE FOUR SEASONS

Pictured on the next page is part of the Court of the Four Seasons, showing the direct lighting from masked batteries of searchlights and the indirect lighting from the veiled standards, giving a soft, subdued, yet brilliant effect.

The half dome and the colonnade in front of the niche of Spring appears with a softness like the evening twilight, a great improvement over the glaring effect heretofore obtained in illuminations.

Over the high wall of the court can be seen the more brilliant Tower of Jewels with its myriads of Novagems or hand-cut jewels. The system of illumination at the Panama- Pacific International Exposition is so perfect that the delicate tints of pink, terra-cotta, Persian blue, and the deeper shade of ultra-marine are shown with the heightened effect of their true color values.

MAIN ENTRANCE TO COURT OF THE FOUR SEASONS

The Illuminated Court of the Four Seasons.

Main Entrance to the Court of the Four Seasons, Illuminated.

PALACE OF EDUCATION

Pictured on the next page is the western facade of the Palace of Education, showing clearly the half dome of philosophy, the two minarets, and the Moorish dome crowning the center of the Palace.

The part of the building shown in the picture fronts on Administration Avenue, skirting the beautiful Fine Arts Lagoon. Its fortunate situation and artistic and clever arrangement of water and shrubbery combine to make this one of the beauty spots of the Exposition. Picturesque islands dot this lagoon.

John McLaren, the Scotchman responsible for the landscaping of the Exposition grounds, is a close student of nature and succeeds in producing a natural rather than a formal effect. He has successfully produced a pocket edition of one of the matchless lochs of his native land with the design of the Fine Arts Lagoon. The Palace of Education was designed by Messrs. Bliss & Faville of San Francisco.

COURT OF ABUNDANCE

The southwest corner of the Court of Abundance is the only example of Gothic architecture in the Exposition. The Court of Abundance, pictured in the spread on the previous page, shows the Oriental influence and the Spanish-Moorish design that was created by Louis C. Mullgardt of San Francisco.

Robt. Aitken's Fountain of Earth is shown in the foreground. The triumphal Arch of the Rising Sun is on the extreme right of the picture, and the Tower of Jewels on the extreme left. This court is dedicated to music, dancing, acting, and pageantry. Shrubs and trees of many varieties and gorgeous flower beds adorn this court.

One can see the orange trees in flower and fruit and smell the delicious perfume from the blossoms as one enters the court. At night the steam and fiery serpents that play their part in the general illumination make a scene at once fascinating and awe-inspiring. Brangwyn's eight great murals have places of honor in this court. Unlike the other courts, the coloring throughout is natural travertine.

COURT OF ABUNDANCE

PALACE OF MANUFACTURES

PALACE OF MANUFACTURES

Pictured on the previous page spread is the southern facade and main south entrance of the Palace of Manufactures. On the right of the picture is shown one of the graceful Italian towers that mark the entrance to the Court of Flowers. In the foreground is one of the many pools scattered over the Exposition grounds, making a perfect landscape.

This particular pool is in front of the Press Building and directly west of Festival Hall. Visitors love to sit and watch the subdued, shimmering reflections of the surrounding palaces and grounds as they find themselves mirrored in the wonderfully clear water.

The Palace of Manufactures is one of the eight central exhibit palaces, and the long Mission facade is broken by the Italian doorway, as shown in the picture, giving these eight palaces the appearance of a great walled city. Messrs. Bliss & Faville are the designers.

This view shows the Palace of Manufactures from the Avenue of Palms. Within its walls are smaller palatial structures, elaborate booths, and exhibit pavilions, in which are displayed the finest fabrics and manufactured goods of every description. The products of the loom from all countries form one of the most extensive displays among the great diversity of lines of manufactures exhibited.

South Portal, Palace of Liberal Arts.

PALACE OF AGRICULTURE

The Palace of Agriculture includes many of the most elaborate exhibits at the Exposition. Nothing more beautiful and interesting could be conceived than the exquisite centerpiece occupying the center of the two main aisles. It represents a typical American farm in four seasons, being so arranged that the spectator sees but one season at a time.

The palace has wonderful exhibits of farm products, modern farm machinery, and all the scientific appliances for extracting the greatest results from Mother Earth. As agriculture advances, so does the civilization of man, and there are many exhibits that entice one to forsake the city for the country.

PALACE OF MINES

The view on the next page is that of the northwest corner of the Palace of Mines and Metallurgy. To the right of the picture is seen part of the northern extension of the very ornate Court of Abundance.

The Palace of Mines and Metallurgy is one of a row of four palaces fronting on the Marina. These fronts form the northern sweep of the walled city, presenting when viewed from either end, an almost solid appearance, being broken only by the extensions of the three main courts. The entrances to these four palaces are repetitions in point of architecture. They are very beautiful and remind one of the entrance to an old-world minster or cathedral.

This northern wall was designed by Messrs. Bliss & Faville of San Francisco. The portion of the Court of Abundance showing on the right of the picture is the work of Louis C. Mullgardt of San Francisco. The distance from the ground to the minaret shown in the center of the picture is 120 feet.

THE AVENUE OF PROGRESS

The facing page shows a view looking down the Avenue of Progress towards San Francisco Bay. The Marin Hills can be seen in the distance. To the right is the main entrance to the Palace of Machinery. On the left is the magnificent facade of the eastern end of the Palaces of Varied Industries and Mines and Metallurgy.

The picture shows one of the everyday crowds common to the Exposition. Day after day, week after week, the Exposition brings increasing numbers of visitors from all parts of the earth. This avenue is the main artery of travel at the east end of the group of exhibit palaces and forms a dividing line between the palaces and The Zone, or amusement section.

ADMINISTRATION AVENUE

The next page features a lovely view looking northward along Administration Avenue towards the California Building, the tower of which can be seen in the distance. The foreground of the picture is almost directly under the great half-dome of Philosophy on the Palace of Education.

The avenue follows the facades of the Palaces of Education and Food Products and marks the western boundary of the great walled city. It is one of the many beautiful walks of the Exposition and, with its wealth of evergreen shrubbery and colorful bunting and flags, presents a very animated scene.

From the delicate pink of the splendid walks to the top of the domes a soft, neutral color scheme of pastel tints has been worked out so successfully that over the entire picture there is not a jarring note. Messrs. Bliss & Faville of San Francisco are the architects of the palaces.

PALACES OF MINES AND TRANSPORTATION

This picture demonstrates in a very striking manner the claim of W. D. A. Ryan, Chief Illuminating Engineer, to "make an illumination as bright as day without the accompanying glare."

Eliminating the background above and below the subject, the picture is not night illumination but rather artificial daylight. One sees the colors as if in the daytime, and the camera records the picture just as readily. The light is bright enough to read the smallest print and yet is restful to the eyes.

The rays of light penetrating the sky are from searchlights on top of the Southern Pacific Company's exhibit. The two palaces shown are, reading from left to right, the Palace of Mines and Metallurgy and the Palace of Transportation, fronting on the Esplanade or Marina, facing San Francisco Bay. If for no other purpose than the demonstration of this new system of illumination, the Exposition will not have been in vain.

COURT OF PALMS

The Court of Palms is one of the two minor courts of the Exposition. The entrance to this court is from the South Gardens and is marked by two of Kelham's Italian towers, each rising to a height of 200 feet. The architecture of this court favors the period of the Italian Renaissance.

The opening in the back of the Court of Palms leads into the Court of the Four Seasons. Standing in the center of this court and looking due north, one can get a very beautiful vista of San Francisco Bay and the Marin hills beyond.

The limpid pool in the center of the court makes the perfect picture, for, it is said, no landscape is really beautiful without the addition of lakes or pools. Wonderful mirrored effects are seen in this pool, especially in the early morning or just before sunset. Instead of the usual evergreens, beautiful palms are planted at intervals throughout this court. Geo. C. Kelham is the designer.

PALACE OF MACHINERY

PALACE OF MACHINERY

The Palace of Machinery is the largest building on the Exposition site. It was designed by Messrs. Wars & Blohme of San Francisco. In architectural type, it is Romanesque.

At the entrance-ways and around the base of the many columns are some wonderful examples of carving and statuary by Haig Paitigian of San Francisco. The four great typical figures surmounting the columns that are repeated on three sides of the palace are, respectively, Steam, Electricity, Imagination, and Invention. These figures are also by Patigian.

The Palace of Machinery is 968 feet long by 368 feet wide and covers approximately seven acres. It forms the eastern boundary of the Exhibit Palace section of the Exposition. The exhibits inside show the wonderful perfection to which various classes of machinery have brought man's ingenuity and are a source of continuous interest and admiration to visitors.

THE AVENUE OF STATES

The imposing building in the foreground is the New York State Building. At the cost of $700,000 for building and maintenance, The Empire State has erected one of the largest and most handsome State buildings on the grounds. The architecture is in the Italian villa style, and it is surrounded by colorful ornamental shrubbery and formal gardens.

At the time the picture was taken, a detachment of the United States Marine Corps was marching past on its way to the Plaza for a daily drill and dress parade. The New York State Building is the host building for all resident New Yorkers, and the visitors from the Empire State can here find social intercourse and abundant hospitality. Besides the State building, there is also a separate municipal building for the City of New York.

THE HAWAIIAN PAVILION

The ornate Hawaiian building is filled with things odd and interesting from the mid-ocean isles. It is situated upon the Marina, at Administration Avenue, near the California and New York State buildings.

WASHINGTON STATE BUILDING

The Washington State building, occupying a block and facing four streets, is a classic design structure, two stories in height, that cost about $50,000. The building is 190 feet long by 80 feet wide, and is divided on the main floor into an exhibit hall and a motion picture hall, with general offices.

On the second floor will be the main social hall, the writing, smoking, retiring and rest rooms for visitors, and display space where fine arts and other exhibits will be shown. In addition to the building, the State of Washington will install elaborate exhibits of the resources, products, and attractions of the state, having a total fund of $175,000 for the exposition work. The exhibits will include forestry, fisheries, horticulture, agriculture and mining, and numerous minor classifications, such as scenery, education, health, and general attractions.

THE OREGON PAVILION

The Oregon Building is a wonderfully imposing structure inspired by the Parthenon at Athens. The forty-eight pillars, five feet in diameter by 40 feet in height, one dedicated to each state in the Union, are immense logs that were contributed by various logging companies of Oregon.

The entire building is from the Oregon forests. There are two floors, the lower having reception, lecture, and exhibit halls. On the second floor and balcony are located the art gallery, dining rooms, and kitchen. The building cost, exclusive of contributed materials, is $60,000.

THE MASSACHUSETTS PAVILION

Among the most revered and best-loved historical structures in Massachusetts is the old Bulfinch part of the State House, facing Boston Common, of which the above is a representation.

THE VIRGINIA STATE BUILDING: WASHINGTON'S HOME AT MT. VERNON

At the Exposition, Virginia has built a reproduction of the home of Washington, at Mt. Vernon, the shrine of the patriots' devotion. In early colonial and revolutionary days, Massachusetts and Virginia stood firmly together, mother states of early presidents.

A peculiar vein of sympathy has always existed between their statesmen and patriotic citizens. A fine sentiment has caused these two old states, bordering the Atlantic, to set up these emblems of their most patriotic regard in the great commonwealth which stretches so far north and south upon the shores of the Pacific.

ADDITIONAL STATE BUILDINGS

Clockwise from the top left: Kansas, North Dakota, Minnesota, New Jersey.

CALIFORNIA BUILDING

The California Building is in the Mission style of architecture, and it was designed by Thos. H. F. Burditte of San Francisco. There is a four-story tower at the northern end of a great court. The court is a reproduction of the famous forbidden garden at the Mission Santa Barbara and is completely surrounded by a two-story building.

The main tower is used as an administration building for the chief executives and officials of the Exposition. This is also the host building of the Woman's Board, an auxiliary of the Exposition. The California Building receives and entertains the notables and generally looks after the comfort and welfare of visitors.

In this building is shown the displays of California's fifty-eight counties that give one a comprehensive view of the resources, industries, and attractions of the great state. This is the second-largest building on the Exposition site and represents in building and furnishings an outlay of $2,000,000.

THE ESPLANADE

ESPLANADE AND MARINA

One can spot the beautiful Column of Progress in the distance beyond the Esplanade pictured in the image on the following page. The Esplanade runs along the northern facade of the walled city composed of the eight main exhibit palaces, dividing it from the broad expanse of lawn fronting on San Francisco Bay known as the Marina.

Along this Marina, immediately northwest of the Column of Progress, is situated the spacious yacht harbor, where the aquatic exercises of the Exposition are to be indulged in. To the left of the picture can be seen a portion of the California Building, and to the right, among the trees, part of the Hawaiian Pavilion.

While walking along this Esplanade, a wonderful marine panorama unfolds itself - The broad grass plots of the Marina, terminating in the low stone coping or sea wall, and beyond, the Bay of San Francisco alive with various craft and, back of all, the purple and green hills of Marin County reaching away to faithful old Tamalpais.

YACHT HARBOR

ITALIAN PAVILION

The Italian group of buildings is one of the finest in the Exposition. The group consists of eight buildings grouped around Piazzas in true Italian style. The buildings are connected with each other by cloisters and represent in their architecture the fourteenth, fifteenth and sixteenth centuries

PALACE OF VARIED INDUSTRIES

ILLUMINATION OF THE TOWER OF JEWELS AND ITALIAN TOWERS

The Chief of Illumination completely discarded the old system of illumination by the stringing of incandescent lights. Instead, the buildings pictured on the next page were illuminated by an elaborate system outlining the shapes of the buildings with small lamps.

By an entirely new system called floodlighting, a soft, restful yet perfect light is thrown over the scene revealing in wonderful clearness every detail of architecture, the color of the shrubbery and flowers, and bringing out with heightened effect the mural paintings and statuary.

At a point near the Yacht Harbor is a giant scintillator that weaves in the night sky ever changing color schemes casting an effect that rivals the Aurora Borealis or "Great Northern Lights."

THE GREAT SOUTH GARDENS

2032. The Chinese Pavilion, Panama-Pacific International Exposition, San Francisco, 1915.

THE DENMARK PAVILION

The Denmark Pavilion occupies a unique position among the foreign pavilions in as much as it has been erected by popular subscription among the Danish-born residents in America. The scheme was initiated by a local committee that has labored strenuously for over five years, being organized for this purpose the very day the exposition movement was launched.

The committee has been working under the patronage of His Majesty, King Christian X of Denmark, and has been augmented with prominent Danes throughout the United States.

THE JAPANESE PAVILION: KINKAKUJI TEMPLE

The reproduction of the famous temple of Kinkakuji of Kyoto is built in the garden of Japan as the social hall of the Japanese Commission. Elaborate arrangements are made by the commission for entertainments and receptions to be held in Kinkakuji.

THE PALACE OF PURE FOODS

ADMINISTRATION AVENUE

ON THE ZONE

This view is one looking west along The Zone, or amusement street. About half of its entire length is shown in the picture, as there is a slight curve to the left about midway through.

As shown in the picture, visitors throng this thoroughfare to such an extent that on many days it is a seething, surging mass of humanity, all bent on having a good time. On both sides of the way, continuously for 3,000 feet, there is a succession of attractive amusement concessions. The entire Zone represents an outlay of more than $10,000,000 and employs in its operation more than 7,000 people.

While being much more elaborate in the preparation of the shows than at other previous Expositions, it is also more refined. The selections have been made not only with a view to their novelty but also their educational value.

SCENES FROM THE SUBMARINE

1. Sunken Spanish Caravel. 2. Amphitrite coming to Neptune. This is a "scenic ride" in a "fac-simile" of the U. S. Government Submarines, through the seas of the universe, visiting different climes and seeing life fathoms below the surface of the ocean. There are visions of Davy Jones's Locker, the beautiful caves of Neptune and his Court, the famous blue grottoes of Capri, the sponge and coral beds of the tropics, and many wonderful sea growths.

"JAPAN BEAUTIFUL"

"Japan" is one of the largest concessions on the Exposition grounds. It embodies actual scenes of Japanese life in the city, country, and villages. The entrance is an exact reproduction of the Daibutsu of Kamakura, the famous statue of Buddha, which is reproduced for the first time in America.

CREATION

Creation is a wonderfully striking and effective portrayal by electrical, mechanical, and scenic devices. Water, vapor, and cloud illusions, combined with lightning flashes, thunder, and tumultuous and subdued musical numbers, all culminate in Creation; inspired by the record in the book of Genesis.

EVOLUTION OF THE DREADNAUGHT

This is a spectacular exhibition about the development of the American Navy accompanied by historic naval battles in which our navy has participated, filled with exciting scenes of action.

The Canadian Pavilion - This beautiful great structure contains elaborate displays showing the wonderful resources of our northern neighbors and their vast country.

Clockwise from top left: The Palace of Horticulture, Administration Avenue between the Fine Arts Palace and Palace of Education, The Avenue of Progress and Palace of Machinery, Palace of Horticulture.

Palace of Varied Industries and Palace of Transportation - The exhibits in the Varied Industries Palace are those such as art pottery, cut glass, jewelry, silver and goldsmiths' wares, clocks, marbles, bronzes, paper hangings, upholstery goods, office, and household furniture. The Palace of Transportation faces the Marina, the Avenue of Progress, and Court of the Universe. It is 618 feet long and 579 feet wide.

Exposition Auditorium - The Exposition Auditorium is a four-story structure of steel and stone that graces the Civic Center of San Francisco. It will be a lasting and beautiful monument to the Panama-Pacific International Exposition. The Exposition management is paying more than one million dollars for its erection, and the City and County of San Francisco are paying more than one million dollars for the site. The main auditorium will accommodate twelve thousand persons.

The Philippine Pavilion - The products, food, and industries of the Philippines are shown by various methods.

THE END OF THE TRAIL

MANY MORE BOOKS FROM CGR PUBLISHING AT CGRPUBLISHING.COM

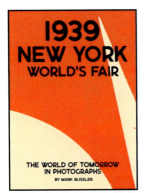
1939 New York World's Fair: The World of Tomorrow in Photographs

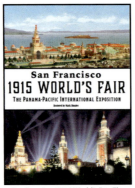
San Francisco 1915 World's Fair: The Panama-Pacific International Expo.

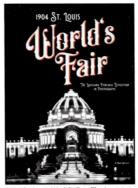
1904 St. Louis World's Fair: The Louisiana Purchase Exposition in Photographs

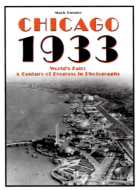
Chicago 1933 World's Fair: A Century of Progress in Photographs

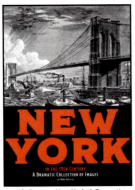
19th Century New York: A Dramatic Collection of Images

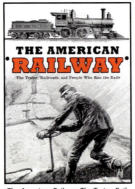
The American Railway: The Trains, Railroads, and People Who Ran the Rails

The Aeroplane Speaks: Illustrated Historical Guide to Airplanes

The World's Fair of 1893 Ultra Massive Photographic Adventure Vol. 1

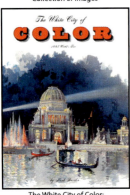
The White City of Color: 1893 World's Fair

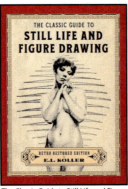
The Classic Guide to Still Life and Figure Drawing

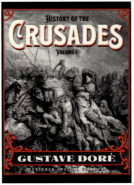
History of the Crusades: Gustave Doré Retro Restored Edition

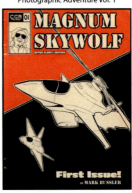
Magnum Skywolf #1

Ethel the Cyborg Ninja Book 1

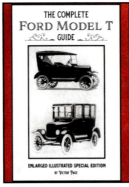
The Complete Ford Model T Guide: Enlarged Illustrated Special Edition

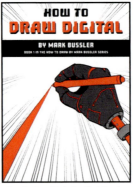
How To Draw Digital by Mark Bussler

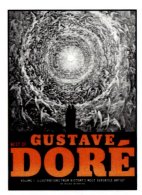
Best of Gustave Doré Volume 1: Illustrations from History's Most Versatile...

MANY MORE BOOKS FROM CGR PUBLISHING AT CGRPUBLISHING.COM

Ultra Massive Video Game Console Guide Volume 1

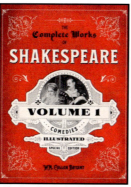
The Complete Works of Shakespeare Volume 1: Comedies Illustrated

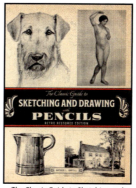
The Clsasic Guide to Sketching and Drawing with Pencils

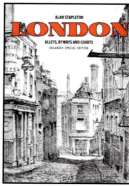
London Alleys, Byways, and Courts: Enlarged Special Edition

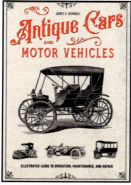
Antique Cars and Motor Vehicles: Illustrated Guide to Operation...

Chicago's White City Cookbook

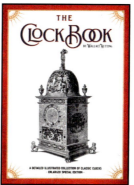
The Clock Book: A Detailed Illustrated Collection of Classic Clocks

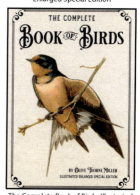
The Complete Book of Birds: Illustrated Enlarged Special Edition

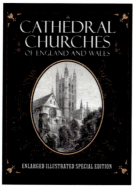
The Cathedral Churches of England and Wales: Enlarged Illustrated Special Ed.

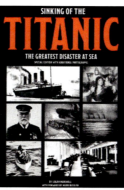
Sinking of the Titanic: The Greatest Disaster at Sea

Gustave Doré's London: A Pilgrimage: Retro Restored Special Edition

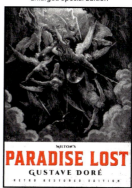
Milton's Paradise Lost: Gustave Doré Retro Restored Edition

The Art of World War 1

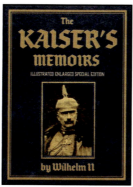
The Kaiser's Memoirs: Illustrated Enlarged Special Edition

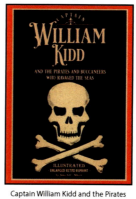
Captain William Kidd and the Pirates and Buccaneers Who Ravaged the Seas

The Complete Butterfly Book: Enlarged Illustrated Special Edition

- MAILING LIST -
JOIN FOR EXCLUSIVE OFFERS

www.CGRpublishing.com/subscribe

Made in the USA
Columbia, SC
26 March 2024

5cab19fa-ecd5-48f8-b418-1e8f11fa1b3cR01